# CHRISTOPHER DAWSON
A Biographical Introduction

# CHRISTOPHER DAWSON

# A Biographical Introduction

### Karl Schmude

Christopher Dawson Centre for Cultural Studies
Hobart, Tasmania

Christopher Dawson Centre for Cultural Studies

The Christopher Dawson Centre for Cultural Studies seeks to encourage critical reflection and research on the history, literature, philosophy and theology that characterise Christian civilisation and culture, in order to raise the profile of these vital disciplines in intellectual life. These humane studies remain an essential key to the full and mature understanding of the underlying currents of Australian life as we strive to hold fast to that synthesis of Faith and Reason that has been gifted to the world by the Christian Tradition.

The Centre was officially launched in Hobart on April 10, 2014, by the former Deputy Prime Minister of Australia, the Hon. Tim Fischer. The Archbishop of Hobart, the Most Rev Julian Porteous, is the Patron of the Centre, and the inaugural Director is Dr David Daintree, formerly President of Campion College Australia in Sydney.

All rights reserved.

First published in 2014 by the Christopher Dawson Centre for Cultural Studies. Revised edition 2022.

Copyright 2014 Karl Schmude.

Front cover image: Christopher Dawson. Drawing by Helen Hull Hitchcock, St Louis, Missouri USA.

www.dawsoncentre.org

ISBN 978-0-6455993-2-9

# Contents

| | |
|---|---:|
| Introduction | 1 |
| Childhood in a Religious Culture | 3 |
| The Oxford Experience | 9 |
| The Life of Cultures | 16 |
| Christianity and European Unity | 22 |
| The Rise of the Mass Culture | 29 |
| An Educational Challenge | 35 |
| Teaching at Harvard | 43 |
| The Closing Years | 50 |
| The Dawson Legacy | 53 |
| Further reading | 57 |
| Endnotes | 59 |

# *Introduction*

THE YEAR WAS 1940, and the continent of Europe was once again convulsed with war. In July, a shy historian was appointed in London as editor of a long-established Catholic journal, *The Dublin Review*. Soon afterwards, he was asked by the Archbishop of Westminster, Cardinal Hinsley, to help lead an English ecumenical group called The Sword of the Spirit.

Few tasks could have seemed more remote from the hostilities that were engulfing the people of England at that time. Yet in the years that followed, Christopher Dawson inspired a new understanding of the Second World War. Drawing on his vast knowledge of history, he went to the spiritual and cultural heart of the conflict. In his first editorial, he wrote:

> 'England and the whole world are passing through a terrible crisis. We are fighting not merely against external enemies but against powerful forces that threaten the very existence of our culture... For the present conflict is not just a material struggle for markets and territory, it is a battle for the possession of the human soul.'[1]

By 1940, Dawson had established a substantial reputation as a cultural historian, and was widely applauded by figures as diverse as T.S. Eliot, Arnold Toynbee and David Jones. When Eliot was asked in America in the 1930s who was the most powerful intellectual influence in England at that time, he responded: 'Christopher Dawson.'[2]

Yet Dawson was not a conventional historian, absorbed by a particular period or personality. Rather, in the words of his lifelong friend, E.I. Watkin, he was, first and last, 'an interpreter: interpreter of human culture in general but more particularly of Christian culture.'[3]

In the years of World War II, Dawson was engaged in nothing less than a rescue mission—but one that enlisted intellectual and spiritual resources rather than military arms. The atmosphere of the time was intense, even apocalyptic, but Dawson showed no sign of panic. On the contrary, his writings brought poise and perspective to the prevailing frenzy. As a fellow Catholic writer, Bernard Wall, remarked: 'in the general hysteria of the time,' Dawson 'went on calmly disentangling the sociological threads in Europe.'[4]

During those testing years, we may be inclined to wonder, was Dawson conscious of the contrast between the turmoil of war and the peacefulness of his boyhood background? Did he ponder the early experiences which helped to guide and fortify him for his wartime mission, and his lifelong vocation as an historian of religion and culture?

# Childhood in a Religious Culture

CHRISTOPHER DAWSON GREW up in an environment sharply different from the chaos of a continent at war. He was born fifty years earlier—on October 12, 1889—in the Welsh village of Hay-on-Wye, which lies in the borderland between Wales and England. The location proved symbolically important, for Dawson lived intellectually all his life in the borderlands—studying the interaction between religion and culture and blending the insights of various disciplines in an effort to produce a balanced picture of historical and contemporary realities.

From his family he inherited a powerful religious tradition. On his father's side, he descended from a Yorkshire family that was military and landowning, and on his mother's, from a Welsh background, but both represented what E.I. Watkin aptly called 'the pre-eminently gracious and cultured tradition of the Anglican country gentleman.'[5]

Dawson described this heritage in later essays, particularly 'The World Crisis and the English Tradition' (1933),[6] in which he explained how the English way of life was built on the natural foundations of the family and the land, and 'Tradition and Inheritance: Reflections on the Formative Years' (1949), which offered a remarkably personal insight into the religiously inspired culture that shaped Dawson's sensibility. His abiding memory of childhood was 'the power of religion, still deeply rooted in the social life I knew—a massive, objective, unquestioned power that impressed its seal on the outer and the inner world alike and held past and present together as a living whole.'[7]

Following his early upbringing in Wales, Dawson moved to Yorkshire after his father's retirement from the army. It was from his father, an Anglo-Catholic, that he imbibed his Catholic sympathies and his view of history. In Yorkshire his earliest impressions were reinforced and extended by his social immersion in a Christian culture.

Sketching the setting of Dawson's life in Yorkshire, E.I. Watkin saw the physical aspects of a hill overlooking a stream as reflective of deeper realities:

> '[T]here the softer beauty of the lower grass slopes is framed by vast expanses of moorland, [which] seems to me typical of the spirit of that cultured tradition—a fair civility of learning and gentle manners embedded in and supported by the infinite prospect of religious faith.'[8]

A vital part of Dawson's sensibility was his love of landscape, and nowhere is this more vividly captured than in the memoirs of his childhood. He cherished a lifelong impression of the harsh beauty of the Yorkshire countryside, and revealed his exceptional awareness of the natural world:

> 'Yorkshire was a new world and the whole aspect of the country with the stone walls climbing the hills and the naked rock thrusting itself out in great scars and promontories, like sea cliffs, was entirely unlike anything I had seen before.'[9]

Thus Dawson experienced at first hand the pervasive importance of religion—that it 'was not simply concerned with the pious moralities which held such a prominent place in Victorian books for children, but stood close to that wonderful non-human world of the river and the mountain which I found around me.'[10]

Apart from the religious culture that Dawson imbibed, he was blessed with a rich blend of other parental influences. From his father, he received an appreciation of mysticism, philosophy and the classics, and from his mother, a love of poetry.

At the age of six, he wrote his first literary composition, an allegorical story about a battle between the Christians and the heathens—a remarkable prefigurement of the religious imagination and cultural intuition which he brought to his later historical studies.

### BOOKS AND IDEAS

In 1899, Dawson was sent to a preparatory school. This proved to be a miserable institutional experience by comparison with the contentment of his secluded childhood. Dawson was by nature intensely shy and never at ease in crowded social settings like a school—or later, a lecture theatre. Yet he warmed to individual people and relied on the stimulation of personal friendships. 'Conversation is more than bread and meat to me,' he once confided to his friend Watkin. 'I cannot exist without it.'[11]

After four years, he moved to one of Britain's oldest public schools, Winchester College. While it embodied many of the uncongenial features of his preparatory education, it offered the compensation of a strong religious tradition and communal purpose.

Dawson was devoted to books from an early age—a reflection of family influence and the relatively undistracted nature of rural life—but during this period, at the age of 15, he began to read extensively. His interests were as diverse as Greek philosophy, Christian mysticism, art, poetry and modern novels.

A lifetime practice of constant reading was supported by the habit of collecting books, and Dawson gradually built a personal library of many thousands of volumes. When he was later appointed to a Chair at Harvard University, he transported a significant part of his library to his campus residence in Massachusetts. His publisher, Frank Sheed, pointed out that Harvard already had a vast library, to which Dawson simply replied: 'Books are my tools.' As a good carpenter, Sheed realised, Dawson needed 'a full kit of books.'[12]

His personal library signified that the main adventure of his life was intellectual. He inhabited above all the world of ideas. His life was marked by a continuing breakthrough of ideas, which led to a continuing flow of books. 'He lived,' as Frank Sheed commented, 'more wholly in the mind than anyone I ever met.'[13]

A special benefit of attending Winchester College was the opportunity to experience the religious radiance of the nearby cathedral:

> 'I learnt more during my school-days from my visits to the Cathedral at Winchester than I did from the hours of religious instruction in school. That great church with its tombs of the Saxon kings and the mediaeval statesmen-bishops gave one a greater sense of the magnitude of the religious element in our culture and the depths of its roots in our national life than anything one could learn from books.'[14]

## EXPERIENCE OF A CATHOLIC CULTURE

Dawson's health was always delicate, and after continuing bouts of bronchitis he left Winchester College and spent several months recuperating in Switzerland.

While on the Continent he visited Rheims Cathedral and was greatly impressed by his first experience of Catholic worship and the culture of popular Catholicism. At Strasbourg Cathedral, he was struck by how readily the rich and the poor seemed equally at ease in the house of God: there were fashionable ladies and ragged beggars, and children lighting candles before a favourite saint. It was an impression of organic vitality that contrasted with the more orderly and respectable behaviour of English congregations, and it enlivened Dawson's appreciation of a Christian people, the *plebs Christiana*, which informed so many of his historical works.

In particular, Dawson saw in Europe the integrated life of a religious culture. He observed at first hand the creative intermingling of a popular culture of spiritual devotions and social practices and a 'high' culture of intellectual penetration and artistic expression. When he later came to analyse intellectual movements in history, he did not neglect the spiritual and social traditions by which they were nourished—as when he noted that the Catholic revival of the 19th century was made possible 'by the survival of a living Christian tradition among the masses,' or when he gauged the importance of Rousseau in the 18th century, with his democratic ideology of the rights of man, as supplying the emotional dynamism which turned the philosophical insurgency of the Enlightenment into a mass movement of social and political revolution.[15]

In 1906, Dawson went to study under private tutors—as a continuing preparation for university. The first was the Rev. C.H. Moss, Rector of Bletsoe in the county of Bedfordshire, where he met E.I. Watkin. Together they found the educational experience of a private tutor 'a short intense interlude in their boyhood and one neither of them ever forgot.'[16]

The second exposure to private tutoring was in Oxford and Germany. Dawson spent several months in Germany, and while he struggled to master the language, he developed a keen admiration of German culture—its philosophy, poetry, music and Baroque churches—but an equivalent distaste for its scrupulous indifference to religion. 'People get on so very well without religion …,' he wrote to his sister. '[T]hey examine Christianity as if it was a kind of beetle.'[17]

This early experience may have served to prepare him for the massive secularisation he was to study as a rapidly growing condition in Western society. In the role of a practising historian, he would spend his life illuminating this condition—the great divorce between religion and culture, between 'the spiritual life of the individual and the social and economic organisation of modern culture.'[18] Though in many ways a quintessential Englishman, formed in the provincial mould of a religious and rural culture, Dawson was exposed early to broader influences, the philosophical and religious maelstrom of a transformed Europe. This prepared him for an appreciation of urbanised and divided cultures, and an interpretation of history that transcended secular versions which assumed no higher meaning than the material—or no wider meaning than the national.

# The Oxford Experience

In 1908, DAWSON entered Oxford University, attending the same college—Trinity—as John Henry Newman almost a century before. In time, they were often to be compared, in regard to their personalities, breadth of learning, and religious and cultural impact; but, at Oxford, they had quite different experiences.

Unlike Newman, Dawson did not relish his education at the University, owing mainly to his shyness and a lack of interest in the set history syllabus. He did, however, enjoy the advantage of studying under a gifted tutor, Ernest Barker, who encouraged the widest range of reading and had expertise in certain areas—notably, medieval studies and the philosophy of history—which greatly interested Dawson. Years later, Barker reviewed a Dawson book and remarked on how much he, the teacher, had learned from his pupil, both at Oxford and in subsequent years.[19]

While the Oxford experience did not mean a great deal educationally to Dawson, it had other effects. It yielded singular memories, particularly of the historical environment of the colleges and the beauty of a city and the surrounding countryside, which Dawson always treasured. It also reaped two benefits of immeasurable importance. One was the meeting with his future wife, Valery Mills. Dawson was only 19, and several years were to pass before they became engaged (in 1913) and finally married (in 1916); but Valery's lifelong care of him was vital—and especially her bearing the practical burdens of the household which allowed him to concentrate on his writing. In Watkin's words, 'she stood between him and the material shocks of daily life.'[20]

### DEEPENING OF FAITH

A second benefit of the Oxford experience was that it stimulated the contemplation of Dawson's own religious faith. His family heritage had indeed nurtured this faith profoundly, but it did not prevent a phase of adolescent wavering. By the time he came to university, however, he had returned to the Anglo-Catholicism of his youth. His faith soon deepened, partly due to his becoming more familiar with the 19th century Oxford Movement, and especially Newman's writings, and partly as a result of a visit he made to Rome in 1909 during an Easter vacation from Oxford.

His first experience of Rome came 'as a revelation' to him. It unfolded 'a new world of religion and culture.' In a later reflection on his conversion, entitled 'Why I Am a Catholic,' he elaborated on this 'new world':

> 'I realised for the first time that Catholic civilisation did not stop with the Middle Ages, and that contemporary with our own national Protestant development there was the wonderful flowering of the Baroque culture.... .
> 
> 'To me at least the art of the Counter-Reformation was a pure joy, and I loved the churches of Bernini and Borromini no less than the ancient basilicas. And this in turn led me to the literature of the Counter-Reformation, and I came

to know St Teresa and St John of the Cross, compared to whom even the greatest of non-Catholic religious writers seem pale and unreal.'[21]

Another factor in the deepening of Dawson's faith at this time was St Augustine's *City of God*, which exerted a powerful influence on his mind—particularly his religious ideas. In Dawson's judgment, Augustine was 'a profoundly original genius.' He changed the history of his time and left for later generations an immense philosophical heritage, covering the Christian interpretation of history as well as Western mysticism and ethics.[22] In Dawson's writings, references to Augustine abound, but his most substantial study was two essays he contributed to a 1930 collection, *A Monument to St Augustine*.[23]

Part of Augustine's appeal for Dawson was possibly his position between two historical ages, a bridge between the passing classical world and the new medieval order struggling to emerge. In his various reflections on Western culture in the 20th century, Dawson often characterised it in those terms—an old order disintegrating and a new culture yet to be born. It was a crisis in which he found the faith and understanding of Augustine to be uniquely instructive.

To a decisive extent, Dawson may qualify as a new Augustine for our age, and his entire work, as the English Dominican Aidan Nichols noted, 'is best thought of as a latter-day *City of God*.'[24]

CONVERSION TO CATHOLICISM

Despite the quickening of interest in Catholicism during his Oxford period, Dawson's conversion did not take place for a further two years. It was, most decidedly, a development, not a denial, of his early religious formation—a movement towards embracing the universal Christianity of the Catholic Church without repudiating the positive values and traditions of his religious past.

The turning point was his systematic reading of the Bible:

> 'It was by the study of St Paul and St John that I first came to understand the fundamental unity of Catholic theology and the Catholic life. I realised that the Incarnation, the Sacraments, the external order of the Church and the internal working of sanctifying grace were all parts of one organic unity, a living tree, whose roots are in the Divine Nature and whose fruit is the perfection of the Saints.
>
> 'This fundamental doctrine of Sanctifying Grace as revealed in the New Testament and explained by St Augustine and St Thomas in all its connotations removed all my difficulties and uncertainties and carried complete conviction to my mind.'[25]

No longer could Dawson hesitate, even though he foresaw the likely cost in ruptured friendships and family ties. Just after taking his degree, he was received, on the Eve of the Epiphany in January 1914, into the Catholic Church at St Aloysius in Oxford.

Following a period in Sweden and then London, Dawson returned to Oxford for post-graduate study. Ostensibly this was in agricultural economics, at the request of his father who thought it would assist Dawson in the management of the rural properties he would inherit; but the son devoted his time chiefly to the study of religion and history.

When the First World War broke out, Dawson presented himself for army service but was disqualified on health grounds; so he taught history at a Franciscan school in Oxford and began to engage in what he later termed 'fourteen years of isolated study' (1914-28), as a prelude to writing books.[26]

## ISOLATION AND PERSPECTIVE

This very isolation - almost monastic in its separation from social networks and the traditional centres of culture such as cities and royal courts—gave Dawson an unrivalled intellectual perspective. It supplied the mental space and stimulation for him to probe uninterruptedly the historical roots of his own culture, and the vast currents of change then flowing ever more rapidly.

Of special value in his ongoing reading were philosophy and the social sciences, especially sociology and anthropology. His first published writings, in fact, were in these disciplines rather than history. In 1920 he produced an essay on 'The Nature and Destiny of Man,' which revealed the philosophical foundations on which his career as an historian would be built, while also highlighting the immense scope of his learning and an ability to make it intelligible to the general reader.[27]

Dawson's published writings of this period appeared mainly in the British journal, *The Sociological Review*. They gave an early indication of his desire to analyse institutions and movements rather than simply historical events. As Russell Hittinger has pointed out, the approach of the social sciences 'represents something very close to the core of the modern mind,' which is apt to focus on features of social life rather than issues of philosophy and aesthetics.[28]

Similarly, Dawson's study of anthropology strengthened his understanding of the concept of *culture*—a concept that had been enlivened for him by his early upbringing in Wales and Yorkshire, but which he now recognised more fully as the fundamental social reality to be studied.

Dawson felt at home in studying sociology since the early founders (in particular, Comte) did not harbour a prejudice against religion as a social force, while later sociologists (such as Ernst Troeltsch and Frédéric Le Play, who exerted a major influence on Dawson) had a positive appreciation of the cultural value of Christianity.

### HISTORY AND METAHISTORY

Dawson was a pioneer in bringing together different disciplines and synthesising the insights which each afforded. Hence his historical studies are not just a narrative of the past, abounding in isolated facts, but a rich and organic unfolding of human life and history. He realised early that history was not a flat record of events but 'a series of different worlds,' each of which 'had its own spirit and form and its own riches of poetic imagination.'[29]

This was not to discount the importance of empirical research and historical analysis which pick out patterns and connections. But the mastery of such techniques, Dawson argued, 'will not produce great history, any more than a mastery of metrical technique will produce great poetry.' What is needed is a universal vision, founded on the facts of history but not confined to them—a 'metahistory,' in fact, which places the passing of human affairs in a transcendental light, and draws its creative power from insights that have more in common with religious contemplation than scientific generalisation.[30]

Witness his account of the historical contrast between Catholic and Protestant society in the 17th century:

> 'Thus it was on the popular level that the differences between the two cultures are most obvious and their separation is most complete. For what could be sharper than the contrast between the popular culture of Catholic Europe with its pilgrimages and festivals and sacred dramas all centring in the great Baroque churches which were the painted palaces of the Saints, and the austere religious life of

the hard-working Protestant artisan and shop-keeper which found its outward expression in the weekly attendance in a bare meeting house to listen to the long sermons of the Puritan divines and to sing long psalms in metrical but far from poetical versions?'[31]

# The Life of Cultures

IN 1928, DAWSON published his first book, *The Age of the Gods*, a study of prehistoric cultures. He drew on the findings of archaeology and other disciplines to produce a new synthesis of the prehistoric culture of Europe with the archaic culture of Asia. He shed light, not only on the evolution of culture as a common way of life, reflecting man's adjustment to his natural surroundings and economic needs, but especially on the religious basis of culture.

Dawson's original plan was to produce a consecutive history of culture—from its beginnings in prehistory through classical antiquity to the Christian era - and *The Age of the Gods* was to be the first of a projected five-volume work. This was not just an ambitious project, but nothing less than a vocation which Dawson had long nursed, for he believed, as he confided to his diary at the time, that it was God's will he should attempt it.[32]

In 1909, he had gone to the *Ara Coeli*, one of Rome's oldest churches, built on the Capitol and displaying in its interior architecture a compound of cultures, pagan and Christian. This experience dramatised for Dawson the continuity of history and the cultural impact of a transforming Christianity. Sitting on the steps of the Capitol where Edward Gibbon had been moved to write his great study of *The Decline and Fall of the Roman Empire*, Dawson conceived the idea of assembling a monumental study of cultural history—a work which the Australian Catholic poet and essayist, Martin Haley, described as 'a *Summa* of culture'. [33]

The multi-volume series did not eventuate in that schematic form. It was replaced by a series of individual studies, written over several decades, which illuminated ever more fully the creative interactions of religion and culture in history.

The remarkable consistency of Dawson's thought is shown in his statement in *The Age of the Gods* on the nature of culture:

> 'A culture can only be understood from within. It is a spiritual community which owes its unity to common beliefs and a common attitude to life, far more than to any uniformity of physical type.... .
>
> 'Throughout the history of humanity the religious impulse has been always and everywhere present as one of the great permanent forces that make and alter man's destiny, and the deeper we delve in the past, the more evident it is how inseparable is the religious instinct from human life and society.'[34]

Thus Dawson's first book set the scene for the more than 20 books that followed it. Only by attending to the *inner life* of a culture, whether primitive or civilised, could a full and proper picture of humanity be drawn.

This fundamental insight remained valid, and even later archaeological discoveries have not diminished the ground-breaking achievement of *The Age of the Gods*. The book received many plaudits, including one from the distinguished archaeologist, Professor Gordon Childe, who described it as 'the most comprehensive, most erudite, most sane and consequently most successful effort [in prehistoric studies] that I have come across.'[35]

Dawson's 'fourteen years of isolated study' had found an initial—and triumphant—expression.

#### FAITH AND THE SUBSTITUTES FOR FAITH

*The Age of the Gods* was followed by various books in rapid succession. First came *Progress and Religion* (1929), a remarkable work of historical synthesis in which Dawson showed the idea of Progress as a substitute faith, performing for Western civilisation the function normally supplied by religion. As he wrote:

> 'Every living culture must possess some spiritual dynamic, which provides the energy necessary for that sustained social effort which is civilization. Normally this dynamic is supplied by a religion, but in exceptional circumstances the religious impulse may disguise itself under philosophical or political forms.... .
>
> 'Moreover, the fact that religion no longer finds a place in social life does not necessarily involve the disappearance of the religious instinct. If the latter is denied its normal expression, and driven back upon itself, it may easily become an anti-social force of explosive violence.'[36]

As so often with Dawson, an insight at an early period foreshadowed a later and fuller realisation[37]—as, in the aftermath of World War II and the West's experience of totalitarian powers, Dawson stressed the vital distinction between an ideology and a faith. While an ideology is intended to fulfil the same *sociological* functions as a faith, it does not correspond to a genuine *transcendental* reality—'a higher and more universal range of reality than the finite and temporal world to which the state and the economic order belong.'[38]

Dawson realised that the new totalitarian states drew their

power from the way they replaced the realities of religious faith with the deceptions of ideology, creating historical myths, for example, as a psychological basis of social unity. But finally such myths will not serve the purpose:

> 'When the prophets are silent and society no longer possesses any channel of communication with the divine world, the way to the lower depths is still open and man's frustrated spiritual powers will find their outlet in the unlimited will to power and destruction.'[39]

While *Progress and Religion* marked a departure from the projected five-volume history of culture, it contained a major intimation of what would have constituted the second volume—namely, a chapter on 'The Rise of the World Religions.' Dawson explored various unifying themes evident in the different world religions in China, India, Persia and Greece. Above all was the 'appearance of new spiritual forces which have been active in the world ever since,' such as the connection between ritual practice and moral belief and behaviour.[40]

### CATHOLIC REVIVAL IN EUROPE

Throughout his life Dawson enjoyed independent means, but these were not always sufficient to support his family responsibilities. At different times he took on part-time academic posts, notably that of Lecturer in the History of Culture at Exeter University (1930-36). He also delivered lecture series, such as the Forwood Lectures at the University of Liverpool (1934) and the Gifford Lectures at the University of Edinburgh (1947-48); and he even applied (in 1933) for a full-time Chair of the Philosophy and History of Religion at Leeds University, but in spite of significant academic support was finally rejected on the grounds of his Catholicism.[41]

In 1930, he began editing, in conjunction with Mr Tom Burns (later editor of the London *Tablet*), a series of short books called Essays in Order. In a general introduction, Dawson noted the enormous cultural changes which had destroyed much of value in the traditions of the past but 'also swept away many of the inherited prejudices and fixed forms of thought which isolated the Catholic tradition from vital contact with the realities of modern life.'[42]

The essayists in this series were from various European countries, and reflected the resurgence of Catholic thought then taking place in Europe.[43] Dawson penned two of the volumes, *Christianity and the New Age* (1931) and *The Modern Dilemma: the Problem of European Unity* (1932), as well as contributing introductions to a number of others, including Jacques Maritain's *Religion and Culture* (1931).

The 1930s was an extraordinarily lively period for Catholic intellectual writing, and there was a range of publishing outlets for Dawson—notably, *The Dublin Review* (for which he wrote numerous articles and book reviews prior to his serving as editor from 1940 to 1944), *The Criterion* (edited by T.S. Eliot), and *Colosseum* (edited by Bernard Wall). In the December 1935 issue of *Colosseum*, for example, Dawson contributed one of his most penetrating and prophetic articles, 'Catholicism and the Bourgeois Mind.' He analysed the distinctive character of middle-class religion long evident in Protestant Christianity and destined to manifest itself in Catholic life several decades later, amid the broadening affluence of post-war Western society.

The essay testified to Dawson's maturity, not only intellectually but as a literary stylist. His prose was the servant of his judgments—lucid and balanced, economic yet elegant. In particular, it served as an effective expression of his poetic imagination, as when he contrasted the culture of Catholic Europe with that of Protestant lands in the 17th and 18th centuries:

'It is not merely that [the Baroque culture of Spain and Italy and Austria] was an *uneconomic* culture which spent its capital lavishly, recklessly and splendidly whether to the glory of God or for the adornment of human life. It was rather that the whole spirit of the culture was passionate and ecstatic, and finds its supreme expressions in the art of music and in religious mysticism.

'We have only to compare Bernini with the brothers Adam or St Teresa with Hannah More to feel the difference in the spirit and rhythm of the two cultures. The bourgeois culture has the mechanical rhythm of a clock, the Baroque the musical rhythm of a fugue or a sonata.'[44]

The atmosphere of the 1930s was increasingly tense. The economic disorder of the Great Depression and the political confusion of European nations, particularly Germany just prior to Hitler's ascendancy, gave rise to the temptation to re-enlist Christianity as a binding force for European society. Dawson offered a message of warning, reflecting his clear understanding of the distinction between religion and culture, however much in practice they seemed to be merged and aligned. In the conclusion to *The Modern Dilemma*, he wrote:

'Nothing could be more fatal to the spirit of Christianity than a return to Christianity for political reasons … . It is only a religion that transcends political and economic categories and is indifferent to material results that has the power of satisfying the need of the world… .

'And today [the Catholic Church] still stands as she did under the Roman Empire, as the representative in a changing world of an unchanging spiritual order.'[45]

# Christianity and European Unity

IT WAS THE Roman Empire which Dawson singled out for initial study in his following book, *The Making of Europe: an Introduction to the History of European Unity* (1932). The Empire played a crucial part in forming the unity of Western culture, but it was not the only factor—nor did Dawson see its role in simply secular terms.

The originality of his analysis was threefold. It lay, first, in the emphasis he gave to the barbarian peoples of Northern Europe, who provided the raw material of European unity and the element of native, and later national, loyalty. Dawson was among the first historians to appraise the contribution of the barbarians to the formation of Europe,[46] prompting Aldous Huxley to remark that, as a result of this book, 'The Dark Ages lose their darkness, take on form and significance.'[47]

Secondly, Dawson recognised the continuities as well as the changes in historical life, and could see through the chaos of those early centuries to a new purpose and order germinating below. He made clear, for instance, that the universal mission of secular Rome harmonised with the missionary ideals of the new Christian religion. Quoting the Christian writer Prudentius, that 'the Roman peace ... prepared the road for the coming of Christ,' Dawson revealed the ways in which a temporal development provided a providential preparation for a spiritual advance.[48]

Finally, Dawson brought together the different threads of cultural life - the Greek and Roman traditions, intellectual, social, institutional and organisational, and the contributions of the barbarians—and showed how the Catholic Church supplied the spiritual dynamic and direction for a new cultural synthesis.

In *The Making of Europe,* Dawson once again covered an immense sweep of history. His lifelong habit of taking long walks—in the country when he occupied his ancestral home in Yorkshire (in the 1930s), or lived near Oxford (1940s), or by the sea during his time in Devon (1950s and later) - almost seems to have been a physical counterpart and stimulus to his intellectual breadth, and his ability to roam over such a vast landscape of learning.

The book is also notable for its blending of general insights with concrete illustrations. In fact, it contains an array of pictorial illustrations, each accompanied by a scholarly description of the scene depicted. Despite poor eyesight, Dawson possessed a powerful visual imagination, and the images revealed his skill in reanimating the past for a new generation.

While the urbane authority of his prose was not matched by a commanding voice in person—as a former student of his, Fr C.J. McNaspy SJ, noted, Dawson was 'always better to read than to listen to'[49]—the robustness of his mind made up for the frailty of his body. Indeed, the richness of his thought could have equipped him, had television documentaries then existed, to present a series like Kenneth Clark's *Civilisation* (1969), for Dawson would have extended the public understanding of Christianity and culture by revealing the impact of religious faith, not only on art and architecture, but on social phenomena such as institutions and movements and the whole process of organic growth and change in the life of peoples.

*The Making of Europe* proved to be a book of enduring

significance and value. It has been frequently reprinted and translated into various languages. In the 1960s, major excerpts appeared in teaching booklets produced by mainstream publishers for American college students - thereby reflecting Dawson's status as a scholar who could condense an historical period or event in a way that illuminated its key issues.[50]

In company with his flow of publications at this time, Dawson also spoke at an important international conference. Travelling to Rome in late 1932, he delivered an address on 'The Interracial Cooperation as a Factor in European Culture.' The audience included prominent Nazis, Goering and Rosenberg, who could hardly have cheered at Dawson's rejection of racial purity. He criticised 'the fanaticism of the modern pan-racial theorists ... who infuse an element of racial hatred into the political and economic rivalries of European peoples,' and commented that, 'if we were to subtract from German culture ... all the contributions made by men who were not of pure Nordic type, German culture would be incalculably impoverished.'[51]

### ESSAYS AND THE OXFORD MOVEMENT

In 1933, Dawson published two books. The first was a collection of miscellaneous essays entitled *Enquiries into Religion and Culture.* Its scope and depth defy any attempt to capture its content adequately. The book contained his first published work, 'The Nature and Destiny of Man,' as well as substantial pieces as diverse as 'The Passing of Industrialism,' 'Christianity and Sex,' 'The Mystery of China,'[52] and 'Islamic Mysticism'.

Dawson's prophetic insight was especially apparent in his long essay on 'Christianity and Sex.' He perceived that the sexual license of the 1920s and its expression in literature were essentially an attack on the family, and the increasing use of contraception—long before the Sexual Revolution of the

1960s and the advent of the Pill—would have a profoundly weakening effect on marriage. He even predicted the 'population implosion' which has come to pass in contemporary Europe, in which the older population strains would cease to reproduce themselves and give way to migrant peoples.[53]

Similarly, Dawson's analysis of Islam—not only his essay on Islamic mysticism but chapters on Muslim culture in *The Making of Europe* and later books—has a remarkably contemporary ring, revealing his understanding of a major world faith that carries heightened urgency for the 21st century.

He skilfully analysed the affinities between Christianity and Islam, including the significance of a tradition of sacred learning—in the Bible and the Koran—and the primacy of religious rather than political citizenship in both cultures. These were characteristics which found expression in the poetry of each faith as well as the lives of their respective saints. But he also identified the differences, citing Islam's lack of a sacramental system and of a belief in a personal mediator between God and man.[54]

Dawson's second book in 1933 was *The Spirit of the Oxford Movement*, which he wrote in honour of its centenary. It was a slender volume which belied the significance of its subject matter and the breadth of the author's view. He did not focus only on England but took account of the broader currents of European intellectual history. He noted, on the one hand, that the Tractarians were embroiled in the religious crisis of the 19th century, as they were contemporaries, not only of Matthew Arnold, but of German thinkers like Strauss and Feuerbach and French philosophers such as Comte and Renan; and on the other hand, Hurrell Froude was influenced by Lamennais and other leading Catholic figures in France.[55]

Dawson could write with personal authority on the Movement as he was brought up in the ambience of its traditions,[56] but he also had—he was now nearly 45—the perspective of mature judgment. When he described this 19th century English culture, with 'the English mind ... more adventurous, more alive to ideas, less stodgy and provincial ... ,' and noted Cardinal Newman's 'imaginative power and intellectual subtlety,' he might almost have been pinpointing the cast of his own mind.[57]

An example of this power and subtlety in Dawson was his realisation that religious life needs a strong intellectual foundation, for without such roots it is prey to the seduction of false ideas—such as the Modernist movement in the Catholic Church in the late 19th century (which assumed great significance in the late 20th century), and the current assault on the Christian faith by a new generation of atheists (as highlighted by best-selling books like Richard Dawkins' *The God Delusion*).

### PROPHETIC SPIRIT AND INSIGHT

The other comparison of importance with Newman is the prophetic spirit they shared, especially in relation to the cultural transformations taking place in their respective times. Dawson and Newman both recognised the essential character of the challenges facing contemporary Christianity. Dawson described Newman as 'the first Christian thinker in the English speaking world who fully realised the nature of modern secularism and the enormous change which was already in process of development, although a century had still to pass before it was to produce its full harvest of destruction.'[58]

Dawson inherited that 'full harvest,' which was the supreme power of totalitarian tyranny. But his own prophetic insight, in the chaos of the mid-20th century, was to recognise that nothing less than the spiritual identity of Christianity and the survival of Christian civilisation were at stake:

'Thus the issue is not simply one between two rival economic or political systems; it involves a spiritual issue that is deeper and more complex. It is the choice between the mechanized order of the absolute State, whether it be nominally Fascist or Socialist, and a return to spiritual order based on a reassertion of the Christian elements in Western culture.'[59]

### SECULAR FUNDAMENTALISM

By the opening of the 21st century, Dawson would doubtless have been alive to a new form of secularism in Europe. It is taking the form of a secular fundamentalism, even totalitarianism, which is not neutral towards religion—and particularly Christianity—but is ideologically hostile to its influence in public life. Here, too, Dawson would assuredly have recognised another manifestation of the 'harvest of destruction,' as shown in the attempt to exclude, in the Constitution of the European Union, all reference to the Christian heritage of European civilisation.

In 1934, Dawson gave a number of guest lectures, including the Forwood Lectures at the University of Liverpool, which found publication in *Medieval Religion and Other Essays* (1934) and later, in an expanded form, in *Medieval Essays* (1953). These writings offered a comprehensive view of the mainsprings of civilisation during the Middle Ages.

This did not mean that Dawson held an unduly rosy view of this long period of history. He knew that its undoubted cultural achievements—such as the construction of the Gothic cathedrals and the creation of universities, the philosophy of Thomas Aquinas and the poetry of Dante—did not insulate it against the flaws of human nature.

Indeed, Dawson did not idealise any period of history, Christian or non-Christian. Like the 19th century Lutheran historian, Leopold von Ranke, Dawson thought that 'every age stands in immediate relation to God.'[60] He possessed a breadth and honesty of mind by which he judged each age on its merits, acknowledging its weaknesses and limitations as well as its efforts and accomplishments. Thus he saw, as he wrote in *The Modern Dilemma*, that the medieval synthesis of religion and culture, while 'it gave a more complete expression to the social function of Christianity than any other age has done, ran the risk of compromising the other Christian principle of transcendence by the immersion of the spiritual in the temporal order—the identification of the Church and the World.'[61]

Even when appreciating the achievements of a period like the Middle Ages, Dawson did not overstate them—or try to minimise the pagan or secular forces which opposed the Church and were not conducive to Christianisation. Thus he pointed out:

'The Middle Ages were not the ages of Faith in the sense of unquestioning submission to authority and blind obedience. They were ages of spiritual struggle and social change, in which the existing situation was continually being modified by the reforming energy and the intellectual activity that were generated by the contact between the living stream of Christian tradition and the youthful peoples of the West.'[62]

# The Rise of the Mass Culture

As the 1930s advanced, Dawson came to be increasingly absorbed by the political and ideological disputes that were gathering force.[63]

His next two books gave voice to these intense preoccupations. The temper of the times was not congenial to the independent thinker trying to distinguish the strands of truth in the midst of polarised loyalties. Yet *Religion and the Modern State* (1936) and *Beyond Politics* (1939) did not reflect any weakening of historical perspective on Dawson's part, nor did they constitute a simple treatment of the political crises of this turbulent decade.

Dawson probed the changing social structures, and emphasised the trend towards a mass culture far more socialised and standardised than before. His writings at this time involved the harnessing of historical insights as a service to cultural understanding and communal preparedness.

Dawson realised that the menace of a mass culture was not confined to Communist or Fascist States like Russia or Germany, but extended to the Western democracies as well. He believed this would follow 'a parallel line of development ... which, while being less arbitrary and inhumane than the other two forms of government, will make just as large a claim on the life of the individual…'[64] Again, the voice of the prophet could be heard:

> 'Never before in the history of the world has a civilization been so completely secularised, so confident in its own powers and so sufficient to itself as is our own…
>
> 'The State of the future will be not a policeman, but a nurse, and a schoolmaster and an employer and an officer—in short an earthly providence, an all-powerful, omnipotent human god—and a very jealous god at that. We see one form of this ideal in Russia and another in Germany. It may be that we shall see yet a third in England and America.'[65]

Three years passed before *Beyond Politics* appeared, chiefly because Dawson fell seriously ill, suffering from various ailments of the heart and spirit—including severe depression, a condition which plagued him periodically throughout his life but was especially acute during this time of social and political tumult.

In publishing *Religion and the Modern State*, he admitted that the prevailing situation was so grave that it had forced him, 'almost against [his] will,' to write the book.[66] While his health was always uncertain, he was tenacious in his convictions. As Bernard Wall testified, in upholding the principles of our existence and coping with the trials and crucifixions of our time, Dawson 'had the heart of a lion.'[67]

*Beyond Politics* took up where *Religion and the Modern State* left off. It laid bare the true nature of the new powers—that they were 'totalitarian in a higher sense,' going beyond the practical functions of the traditional State to cover the whole of life. They sought, Dawson wrote, 'to be, not merely an association for the maintenance of peace and order and the rights of property, but a spiritual community, a fellowship through which the individual attains a higher and more complete life…'[68]

At the same time, he showed his capacity to rise above the temporal circumstances and articulate a transcendental truth of abiding relevance:

> 'The Church lives again the life of Christ. It has its period of obscurity and growth and its period of manifestation, and this is followed by the catastrophe of the Cross and the new birth that springs from failure.'[69]

### THE NATIONS ARE JUDGED

In 1940, Dawson's appointment as editor of *The Dublin Review* and Vice-President of the Sword of the Spirit movement enabled him to address in a more concerted way the threats then looming—both to the freedom of the individual (which the totalitarian State would absorb) and to the independence of the Church (which it would rival).

Through the pages of the *Dublin Review* and the publications of the Sword of the Spirit, Dawson shed light on the ideas and impulses that had provoked the Second World War. He worked at forging a new alliance of intellectual leaders in Europe—straddling the wartime divisions and assembling German as well as Allied thinkers who shared his vision of a Christian order and his devotion to the recovery of a wounded civilisation. The *Review*, in fact, became 'the one truly European periodical' at that time, 'its contributors united in defence of their common culture.'[70]

Dawson's only book during the War carried a distinctive—and disturbing—title: *The Judgement of the Nations* (1943). The opening chapter was called 'The Hour of Darkness,' and Dawson confessed in the Foreword that the book 'small as it is, ... has cost me greater labour and thought than any book that I have written.'[71]

The work itself has an apocalyptic air about it, as if it had been written in the London underground while the air-raid sirens wailed overhead. A sample of his writing highlights the intensity of conviction and passion he felt at that time:

> 'We are passing through one of the great turning points of history—a judgement of the nations as terrible as any of those which the prophets described. We see all the resources of science and technology of which we were so proud devoted methodically to the destruction of our world.
>
> 'And behind this material destruction there are even greater evils, the loss of freedom and the loss of hope, the enslavement of whole peoples to an inhuman order of violence and oppression. Yet however dark the prospect appears we know that the ultimate decision does not rest with man but with God and that it is not His will to leave humanity to its own destructive impulses or to the slavery of the powers of evil.'[72]

### PRESTIGIOUS LECTURES

Following the War, Dawson was invited to give the Gifford lectures at the University of Edinburgh. This series had developed a prestigious reputation, and Dawson spent three years preparing the lectures. He had the distinction of delivering two sets in successive years, 1947 and 1948, an arrangement which proved fortunate as it allowed him to produce something of a summary of his life's work.

The resulting books crystallised his central themes of, first, the general relationship between religion and culture, published as *Religion and Culture* (1948), and secondly, the special relationship of Christianity and Western culture, issued under the title of *Religion and the Rise of Western Culture* (1950).

A key passage in *Religion and Culture* offered perhaps the clearest and most compelling statement of the insight which animated Dawson's intellectual being:

'Religion is the key of history. We cannot understand the inner form of a society unless we understand its religion. We cannot understand its cultural achievements unless we understand the religious beliefs that lie behind them.

'In all ages the first creative works of a culture are due to a religious inspiration and dedicated to a religious end. The temples of the gods are the most enduring works of man. Religion stands at the threshold of all the great literatures of the world. Philosophy is its offspring and is a child which constantly returns to its parent.'[73]

Such a statement would have been familiar to seasoned readers of Dawson, but the two published volumes of the Gifford Lectures were not a mere replica of earlier works. Dawson continued to read and research, widely and prodigiously, and in each new study of an historical period he revealed fresh insights into the interaction between religious impulses and purposes and the cultural forms in which they found expression.

Writing as he was for people living in a highly secularised society, Dawson emphasised the intimate, indeed intrinsic, historical connection between religion and culture:

'Throughout the greater part of mankind's history, in all ages and states of society, religion has been the great central unifying force in culture. It has been the guardian of tradition, the preserver of the moral law, the educator and the teacher of wisdom.' [74]

Dawson saw the total secularisation of social life in our age as a relatively modern and anomalous phenomenon. A society's attempt to conduct its life without reference to any higher laws or powers 'seems as irrational as for a community to cultivate the earth without paying any attention to the course of the seasons.'[75]

## UNDERSTANDING OF NON-CHRISTIAN CULTURES

It could easily be overlooked, given Dawson's reputation as a Catholic historian, that he commanded such a deep and vibrant knowledge of non-Christian cultures. In *Religion and Culture*, for example, he used evidence from Islam, Hinduism, Buddhism and Egyptian culture to illuminate even more clearly themes he had explored in earlier books—notably in *The Age of the Gods* (1928) and *Progress and Religion* (1929). Thus, he explained the religious and cultural roles performed by prophets, priests and kings, and how these have served, in so many environments, as sources of knowledge about God and organs of social learning and organisation.

When it came to the intermingling of the Christian faith and Western culture, Dawson again brought new understandings to light in his successive studies. He offered familiar points, but also fresh perspectives based on further research and reflection.

Thus, in *The Making of Europe*, he focused on the key components—Roman and classical, Catholic and barbarian—which contributed to the formation of Christian culture in the West and the East; but he highlighted martyrdom as the stronghold of spiritual freedom and a religious ideal which resisted the domination of earthly powers. Fifteen years later, in *Religion and the Rise of Western Culture*, he explored a wider theme of the cult of the saints during the Dark Ages—not only as patterns of moral perfection to be followed but as supernatural powers to be invoked. Nearly two decades further on, in *The Formation of Christendom* (1967), he brought out more fully the roots of divine revelation in the Jewish and Christian traditions (which inspired the development of Western culture), as well as the Catholic concept of a universal spiritual society (which formed the communal consciousness of a Christian people).

# An Educational Challenge

FROM THE OUTBREAK of World War II till the early 1950s, Dawson lived near Oxford. The city was no longer the peaceful haven of his earlier time of residence. Industrial and other changes had made the 'dreaming spires' of Matthew Arnold's memory appear less aspirational. But Oxford had the merit of being centrally located—closer to London and the various intellectual and publishing networks on which Dawson was reliant.

It is noteworthy that he never taught at Oxford University—an institution, in the words of the Benedictine historian, David Knowles, 'which he would have greatly graced.'[76] He continued to work on the margins of academic life, avoiding the institutional pressures and subject specialisms that would have curbed his unusually wide scholarly interests, but nonetheless affected by isolation from the organised centres of learning and collegiality.

When he received the Christian Culture Award in 1951 from Assumption University in Ontario, Canada, Dawson called his acceptance speech "Ploughing a Lone Furrow.' He followed his own line of studies, he said, 'not because I could afford to dispense with the help of others, but simply and solely because the subject to which I have devoted myself—the study of Christian culture—has no place in education or in university studies.'[77]

## HUMANISM AND CHRISTIANITY

By the 1940s, Dawson had come to a clear realisation that the preservation of Christian culture—of a social way of life shaped by the Christian faith, which makes religious belief more credible and moral behaviour more practicable—was critically dependent on education.

He began publishing on this theme in 1943, contributing an introduction to another author's book, M. O'Leary's *The Catholic Church and Education*.

Dawson began by noting that the history of civilisation was inseparable from 'a few great traditions and systems of education which formed the intellectual mould in which the thought and expression of the different world societies were cast.'[78] He then traced the distinctive features of Western education—that its sources were diverse, Greek and Jewish, the classics and the Scriptures, and its tradition was essentially that of Christian humanism.

With his great power of summary, he captured this synthesis in a single sentence:

> 'As humanism initiates man into the community of culture and opens to him the treasures of the thought of the past, so Christianity introduces man to the society of the Spirit, the City of God, and opens to him the divine promise of the future.'[79]

With the war ended, Dawson intensified his efforts to connect the crisis of Western culture with the state of education.

He published two seminal articles on this subject in an international journal—the first, in 1946, 'Education and the Crisis of Christian Culture,' in which he linked the secularisation of culture to the utilitarian character of modern education.

Such an emphasis, he believed, would lead to the exclusion of deeper elements and motives, spiritual and cultural, and thus foster a spirit of secularist conformity among people. In a perverse way, the spread of universal education had made this condition of mass-mindedness worse, for it had served to spread secularisation.

The second article, in 1950, was 'The Study of Christian Culture as a Means of Education.' Here he outlined for the first time a new educational approach—a focus on Christian culture as a dynamic spiritual process in history. The process would begin with a study of its spiritual roots, then trace its organic historical growth, and finally comprehend its cultural expressions and effects.[80]

## EUROPE AS A SPIRITUAL COMMUNITY

These two articles later appeared as the framing chapters—the first and the last—of Dawson's next book, *Understanding Europe* (1952). Its general theme was that Europe is not a political creation but 'a society of peoples,' who have a common heritage of religious traditions and moral values, and whose nations form part of a wider spiritual community.

This may have seemed an exalted and even abstract conception, but Dawson argued that Europe was not a 'natural' culture, united by geographical or racial homogeneity. It was, on the contrary, made up of a widespread and diverse set of races, which in time absorbed alien traditions such as those of the Latin culture of the Mediterranean and the barbarian tribes of Northern Europe. In Dawson's view:

> 'This explains the contradictions and disunity of medieval culture—the contrast of its cruelty and its charity, its beauty and squalor, its spiritual vitality and its material

barbarism. For the element of higher culture did not spring naturally from the traditions of the social organism itself, but came in from outside as a spiritual power which had to remould and transform the social material in which it attempted to embody itself.'[81]

Dawson's vision of Europe has found a contemporary echo in the writings of Pope Benedict XVI, particularly in his book *Europe Today and Tomorrow* (2007). In essays written before his pontificate, he analysed the destruction of the Christian heritage of Europe and recognised the rise of Islam and the religious traditions of Asia as spiritual powers 'in contrast to a Europe that is denying its religious and moral foundations.'[82] Curiously the Pope did not cite Christopher Dawson, but only the two historians with whom Dawson was often compared, Oswald Spengler and Arnold Toynbee, neither of whom embodied a Christian perspective.

### EDUCATIONAL REFORM

In post-war Europe, as 'a society of peoples' disintegrated into hostile nations bent on destroying each other, Dawson turned increasingly to the practical solution of educational reform.

Throughout the 1950s, he advocated the study of Christian culture as a new educational program—and the basis of a new cultural synthesis.

A key ally in this work of extended understanding was an American teacher, John Mulloy. He visited Dawson in Oxford in 1953 and became a vital incentive and channel for Dawson's penetration of a wider world and the promise of a more profound impact. In particular, Mulloy served to focus Dawson's attention on the American higher education scene as the one environment where his educational initiative in Christian culture could best be implemented.

A significant step in the spread of Dawson's reputation outside of Europe was Mulloy's compilation of a large anthology of the historian's writings produced over several decades. Published as *Dynamics of World History* (1956), it is a monumental work—possibly the most impressive single volume of Dawson's writings. It illustrated the full array of his erudition and the sheer force of his intellectual power. As Dermot Quinn commented in an Introduction to the latest edition of this frequently reissued book:

> 'The work of a remarkable scholar in his prime, [*Dynamics*] is stamped with the qualities that characterized [Dawson's] career: elegance of writing, breadth and depth of learning, moral seriousness, a powerful capacity for synthesis.'[83]

These qualities, indeed, exemplified, not only the personal advocate of Christian culture but the subject itself as a new and significant inter-disciplinary study.

### PRACTICAL POSSIBILITIES

Throughout the 1950s, Dawson's proposals were published in a multitude of articles in leading Catholic journals in America, such as *Commonweal*, *Thought* and *America*. They generated widespread debate but met strong resistance from the Catholic educational establishment. This was for several reasons - in part because they threatened to replace, as a unifying principle of study, the accepted philosophy of Neo-Scholasticism with an historical and cultural approach; in part because of the highly inter-disciplinary nature of Christian culture in an academic setting wedded to subject specialisation; and in part because Dawson's emphasis on Christian culture was misconstrued as a glorification of Christian history and tradition—and this at the very time when Catholics in North America and elsewhere were beginning to question the validity and value of a distinctive history and tradition.

What were the practical possibilities and expected results of Dawson's proposals? In his belief, a systematic study of Christian culture would give Christians a living grasp of their own identity—in a way that the more abstract approaches of philosophy and theology, by themselves, would not. It would thereby equip them to cope with the distinctive challenges and temptations of a secularist culture.

Dawson noted a remarkable contrast in the contemporary West—between the pluralism of religion and the uniform character of mainstream culture. While the culture was ostensibly open and diverse, the great mass of people were actually conditioned by the same ideas and influences (which have become, since Dawson's time, even more heightened by the pervasive expansion of communications media, particularly the internet). The behavioural conformities of a mass materialistic culture have had a homogenising impact on popular opinions and values, and added new dimensions of difficulty to any efforts to inspire a religious revival in the Western world.

James Hitchcock has highlighted Dawson's distinction between the religious culture of the mass of the people in the 19th century, which survived the assaults of the Enlightenment and the French Revolution and provided the seedbed for a widespread resurgence of Catholicism in Western society, and the diminished condition of popular religious life in our time, so crushed has it become by the common culture of a secularised society.[84]

As Dawson described the terms of the challenge:

> 'The vital problem of Christian education is a sociological one: how to make students culturally conscious of their religion; otherwise they will be divided personalities—with

a Christian faith and a pagan culture which contradict one another continually.

'... Thus the sociological problem of a Christian culture is also the psychological problem of integration and spiritual health. This is the key issue.... We must make an effort to achieve an open Christian culture which is sufficiently conscious of the value of its own tradition to be able to meet secularist culture on an equal footing.'[85]

Dawson could see signs of hope in the contemporary West. He discerned, for example, a revival of corporate ways of thought and action, which challenged the dominant spirit of individualism and provided a possible basis for a communally supportive faith. He also recognised a growing interest in myth and ritual which reflected a recovery of spiritual consciousness.[86] Like so much in Dawson's intellectual makeup, his sensitivity to myth and ritual was nurtured by his upbringing. He attributed to his parents an understanding of the essential link between 'story' and 'legend,' recalling that he came to know the past 'through the enchanted world of myth and legend' and realised that children 'will always find mythical or heroic figures to satisfy their imagination.'[87]

The most immediate outcome of Dawson's educational advocacy was the establishment in 1956 of a Christian Culture Program at St Mary's College, a women's liberal arts institution in Indiana. The College President, Sister Madaleva, and an Austrian-born convert to Catholicism, Professor Bruno Schlesinger (who had completed a PhD on Dawson), were responsible for this initiative. The Program was an early, and hopeful, sign of Dawson's influence in educational circles. While later re-named Humanistic Studies, it continued as an example of the kind of integrated approach Dawson favoured to the modern study of Christian culture.

In the 1970s, a revival of Catholic liberal arts education occurred in America, leading to the establishment of several colleges—such as Christendom in Virginia, Thomas Aquinas in California, and Thomas More in New Hampshire—which reflected Dawson's ideas in varying degrees without being explicitly conscious of his proposals.

# Teaching at Harvard

DAWSON WAS NOW approaching 70 years of age and could reasonably have foreseen a lessening of activity in his retiring years. But an invitation to become the first occupant of a Professorial Chair in Catholic Studies at Harvard University transformed his expectations—and his life and legacy.

The Chair was established by a Catholic alumnus of Harvard, Chauncey Stillman,[88] in the Harvard Divinity School, and it denoted a serious effort at that time by Harvard's President, Nathan Pusey, to reinvigorate the religious identity of America's oldest university. As Pusey stated in the mid-1950s:

> 'The whole world now looks to us for a creed to believe in and a song to sing. The whole world ... and our young people first of all.'[89]

While it would be an exaggeration to describe these efforts as a 20th century 'Harvard Movement,' similar in scope and impact to the 19th century Oxford Movement, Dawson's appointment was nonetheless part of a deliberate response to the apparent triumph of secularism as the prevailing philosophy of Harvard. In the year of Dawson's appointment (1958), Pusey criticised secularism as a new form of fundamentalism, whose 'noxious influence—noxious ... to spirit, imagination and mind—works among us almost unopposed.'[90]

To be appointed as a Catholic Professor at America's first and most famous Protestant university was sufficiently remarkable. It highlighted Dawson's deeply ecumenical instincts, which he had shown throughout his life - most notably in the Sword of the Spirit movement during World War II—and which he believed were now of vital import as the movement towards Christian unity had reached a decisive stage.[91]

The barriers to unity were not simply theological but cultural. In 1938, for example, Dawson drew attention to the sociological foundations of heresy and schism, arguing that such movements derive their impetus from forces in society more than theological disagreements. He realised that there was a great cultural schism between Northern and Southern Europe, which underlay the theological issues dividing Catholicism and Protestantism, and in a European society animated by religious forces, such cultural tensions inevitably assumed religious forms. Dawson captured the possibilities of resolution in the following example:

> '... [A] statesman who found a way to satisfy the national aspirations of the Czechs in the fifteenth century, or those of the Egyptians in the fifth, would have done more to reduce the centrifugal force of the Hussite or the Monophysite movements than a theologian who made the most brilliant and convincing defence of Communion in One Kind or of the doctrine of the Two Natures of Christ.'[92]

## CHRISTIAN CULTURE AND THE UNIVERSITY

Apart from the ecumenical significance of Dawson's appointment, a second benefit was educational. To have the opportunity, from the prestige of Harvard, to broadcast his ideas on Christian culture across the vast field of American higher education - and particularly Catholic universities and colleges (of which there were well over 200 at that time)—was an unimagined bonus.

Dawson moved to America in September 1958 with a buoyant sense of mission, not only because of the new opening it represented for the promotion of Christian culture, but also on account of America itself. Increasingly, he saw the United States as a place of vision and destiny, and the future of Christendom bound up with the American experience.[93]

This was not a political dream on his part or the giving way to a narrow nationalism. Nor did it reflect an uncritical attitude to contemporary American life: in 1961, for instance, he stirred controversy by describing the US Supreme Court's decisions on the First Amendment, which designates the constitutional separation of Church and State, as 'a bulwark of secularist dogma.'[94]

But Dawson was alive to the exceptional energies of America as a culture that was at once technologically advanced and religiously dynamic - and perhaps the only effective custodian of Western values in the post-war world.

On his 70th birthday in 1959, which was marked by a special celebration at Boston College, Dawson recalled how, at the outset, his eyes had been fixed on Europe and the European tradition, but now he had come to feel it was in America that the fate of Christendom would be decided.

In particular, he perceived the promise of America's young and vigorous Catholic tradition, which had found embodiment in a higher education system that could become the channel of a revivified Christian culture.

### WESTERN CULTURE AND A WORLD SOCIETY

The 1950s were a time when Dawson came to focus, not only on the cultural promise of America, but on the importance of the societies of Asia as well.

He served as the General Editor of a Sheed and Ward series, The Makers of Christendom, and in 1955, edited *The Mongol Mission* (later republished under the title of *Mission to Asia*). This work comprised narratives and letters emanating from the journeys of Franciscan missionaries in Mongolia and China in the 13th and 14th centuries, and represented a direct account of the first contact between Western Christendom and the Far East.

During his years at Harvard, Dawson published several more books which showed both the adaptability of his mind and the continuity of his thought. Just as the menaces of wartime Europe in the 1940s brought forth *The Judgement of the Nations* and a realisation of the need for spiritual recovery if Western culture were to be saved, so the Cold War atmosphere of the 1950s generated a powerful awareness of East-West relations and the emergence of a world society.

In his first work, *The Movement of World Revolution* (1959), Dawson explored the relevance of European history to the revolutionary conditions of present-day Asia. The central chapters had previously appeared in a booklet, *The Revolt of Asia* (1957), which argued that the movements for change in the developing world had arisen in Europe and were stimulated by Western ideas and impulses—in areas as diverse as education, technology and political ideology. Long before terms like 'globalisation' became current, Dawson could see the irresistible momentum towards a world society.

A second book, *The Historic Reality of Christian Culture* (1960), applied the perennial Christian tradition to the contemporary challenges of a secularised culture. Comprising a series of thematic essays, the book sketched the lineaments of a Christian culture—such as its sacramental expressions, in areas as diverse as art, architecture, music and poetry, and its institutional forms such as monasteries, all of which served as channels of access to spiritual realities.

As so often, he crystallised in a single sentence the intersection of religion and culture, describing the distinctive character and impact of Christianity:

> '...[I]n Christianity the tendency to a world-renouncing asceticism coexists with a tendency toward social and cultural activity, and it is the tension of these two forces that has given Christianity its characteristic power to change society and to create new cultural forms.'[95]

Dawson could also offer a rousing vision of hope, as in the conclusion to his chapter 'The Outlook for Christian Culture':

> '... [T]hough the Church no longer inspires and dominates the external culture of the modern world, it still remains the guardian of all the riches of its own inner life and is the bearer of a sacred tradition.
>
> 'If society were once again to become Christian, after a generation or two or after ten or twenty generations, this sacred tradition would once more flow out into the world and fertilize the culture of societies yet unborn.
>
> 'Thus the movement toward Christian culture is at one and the same time a voyage into the unknown, in the course of which new worlds of human experience will be discovered, and a return to our own fatherland—to the sacred tradition of the Christian past which flows underneath the streets and cinemas and skyscrapers of the new Babylon as the tradition of the patriarchs and prophets flowed beneath the palaces and amphitheatres of Imperial Rome.'[96]

## CATHOLIC IDENTITY

Dawson's third book during his Harvard years was, in many ways, a manifesto of his American mission. *The Crisis of West-*

*ern Education* (1961) was the culmination of his heroic efforts to reform Catholic higher education by placing the study of Christian culture at the centre of the curriculum.

His aim was to enliven students' awareness of their own cultural traditions, and thereby buttress their sense of Catholic identity in the midst of a culture dedicated to the temporal rather than the eternal, and to a reliance on soft sentiment and the therapy of indulged emotions rather than hard convictions and the solidity of the real.

During his time at Harvard, Dawson travelled to various parts of America to deliver specially invited lectures. Two were of special significance. The first was an address to the Thomas More Association in Chicago in 1959 on 'Catholic Culture in America,' and the second was the Smith History Lecture in 1960, on 'America and the Secularisation of Modern Culture,' delivered at the University of St Thomas in Houston, Texas.

The Chicago lecture gave a penetrating insight into the social evolution of American Catholicism. Dawson traced the influence of the Irish and other immigrant peoples as they adapted the peasant traditions of the Old World to the urban patterns of the New; and he went on to stress the development of an intellectual culture as a basis of Catholic identity in modern America.

Such a transformation was all the more remarkable when Dawson recalled—as he had more than 20 years before - the origins of those who had transplanted this culture from the Old World to the New:

'If there has ever been a class entirely deprived of the necessary economic foundations of a good life it was the refugees of the great Irish famine, who were forced to escape from the physical death of starvation into the living death of the awful nineteenth-century slums of Northern England and Eastern America. They were forced to live as animals are not allowed to live nowadays. Yet it is to these men that the Catholic Church in England and America owes its strength today: they, even more than the survivors of the age of persecution and the converts of the Oxford Movement, are the true heroes of the faith and the creators of modern English and American Catholicism.'[97]

The Houston lecture, a year later, addressed the historical development of American culture and the religious impulses that shaped this development, alongside the drive for material power and social and technological progress.

Dawson explained the secularising effects of isolating the private world of religious experience from the public order of business and politics. He issued a plea for a recovery of 'this lost spiritual dimension of culture.' It is this which underpins a moral order, and provides the ultimate foundation of society. No society, Dawson ominously concluded, 'which denies it or loses sight of it, can endure.'[98]

# The Closing Years

CHRISTOPHER DAWSON'S TENURE at Harvard was due to last five years, but he suffered a series of strokes which forced him to leave prematurely. In 1962, after four years away, he returned to his home at Budleigh Salterton on the Devon coastline.

His life had, in a sense, come full circle—from a traditional culture in England to the dynamic modernity of New England; from the aftermath of the Oxford Movement to the intimation of a possible 'Harvard Movement'; and back again to the familiar solitude of the individual scholar.

But Dawson's homecoming was clouded by ill health as well as a cultural and religious revolution even greater than he could have predicted. The year he left Harvard marked the opening of the Second Vatican Council. In 1965 it concluded, and in that year, a fellow Professor in the Harvard Divinity School, Harvey Cox, published *The Secular City*. This book not only crystallised the cultural changes that Dawson had foreseen, but it endorsed secularisation with uncritical enthusiasm, assuming the status of an ideological cult. It thus fulfilled what Dawson had earlier defined as the essence of theological Modernism—namely, that 'man is the measure of all things and the spirit of the age is the spirit of God.'[99]

In the years following his retirement, two more books appeared. The first was *The Dividing of Christendom* (1965), which elucidated the period from the 16th century Reformation to the 18th century Enlightenment, and the second was *The Formation of Christendom* (1967), which treated of the sources of Christianity and the development of Christian culture during the Middle Ages.

### LANGUAGE AND THE INCARNATION

Of decisive value were Dawson's final reflections on the nature of Christianity and culture. In the early part of *The Formation of Christendom*, he drew on his knowledge of anthropology to stress the supreme importance of language, recognising it as the gateway to the human world and the symbol of human culture. He then linked this understanding with the fundamental character of Christianity, based as it is on 'The Word Made Flesh,' which elevated the word as an instrument of human communication to the Word as a channel of divine salvation.

While some find the essence of religion in contemplation or mystical experience, Dawson pointed out that this is not Christianity. Rather, as he noted:

> '[Christianity] is a religion of Revelation, Incarnation and Communion; a religion which unites the human and the divine and sees in history the manifestation of the divine purpose towards the human race.'[100]

These last books reflected what E.I. Watkin later stated—that Dawson's most fervent hope was that Catholics would learn about their own cultural traditions and develop a deeper understanding and love of their own identity; and that this would be a gift to 'a secularised and spiritually ignorant world as a remedy for its wounds and sicknesses.'[101]

When Dawson advocated this cause from his Harvard Chair, Watkin suggested, it had some prospect of success. But the revolution in Western society, and in the Catholic Church, during the final years of his life—epitomised in Harvey Cox's consecration of the 'Secular City'—put paid, at least temporarily, to any rapid revival of Christian culture in developed countries.

At the same time, Dawson may be regarded as a precursor of the Second Vatican Council and the resultant efforts to heal the divisions between Christians.[102] He gave sustained emphasis, in a lifetime of writing, to the cause of Christian unity. As Dermot Quinn has observed, the idea—and the word—of 'unity' runs through all of Dawson's work, reflecting a language of harmony and consonance in his historical studies that underlies his 'symphonic sense of history.'[103]

# The Dawson Legacy

CHRISTOPHER DAWSON DIED on 25 May 1970, following what his friend Bernard Wall described as 'a long crucifixion of illness.'[104] It was a fitting coincidence that this was the feast day of St Bede, the first English historian whose most notable accomplishment was to shed light on the life of the English people during the Dark Ages—as Dawson did more broadly twelve centuries later.

Yet his writings continued to appear, due especially to the assiduous efforts of his daughter, Christina Scott. In 1972, *The Gods of Revolution* was published. It was part of Dawson's original project of a five-volume history of culture, and focused on the French Revolution and its aftermath. The work was unusual, as John Mulloy remarked, in providing an extensive analysis of a particular historical episode which lasted only a few years, momentous though they were.[105] Dawson grasped the profound significance of the French Revolution, which he discerned as a spiritual reformation and not just a political and social movement. The Revolution was the fulfilment of that religion of humanity which had been the fruit of 18th century thought. Yet it was not only the child of the Enlightenment but also its destroyer. As he concluded:

> 'The philosophic rationalism of the eighteenth century was the product of a highly civilized and privileged society

which was swept away by the catastrophe of the *ancien regime*. In the salons ... it was easy to believe that Christianity was an exploded superstition which no reasonable man could take seriously. But the same men and women felt very differently when the brilliant society that had worshipped at the shrine of Voltaire was decimated by the guillotine and scattered to the four winds.'[106]

In 1975, *Religion and World History* appeared. Comprising various essays, some of which had not previously been published, this volume was a compendium of Dawson's writings on different world religions, including a major section on Christianity, and on topics dealing with history, secularism and spirituality.

Dawson had long maintained that this was the age of the plough and the harrow, not the time of the harvest.[107] While he did not simplistically declare the present era to be a new Dark Ages, he recognised the transitional—and the troubling—character of our era. His many studies of cultural fermentation—starting with *The Making of Europe* in the 1930s, which traced the silent cultivation of a new Christian culture during the original Dark Ages—shielded him against any expectation of sudden and substantial cultural flowerings.

### IMPACT OF DAWSON'S IDEAS

Yet Dawson may have drawn hope from the impact of his thought, particularly in America where he had laboured in the closing years of his active life. His assistant at Harvard, Daniel Callahan, while not fully in sympathy with his outlook, likened Dawson's influence to that of the leading figures of the Oxford Movement:

'After Newman, Manning and W.G. Ward, Oxford was

never quite the same; perhaps in a somewhat similar sense, after Christopher Dawson, Harvard will never be quite the same.'[108]

Dawson's influence has also been felt as far afield as Australia. More than 30 years after his death, a Catholic liberal arts institution deeply influenced by his ideas was established in 2006 in Sydney. Campion College Australia was inspired, on the one hand, by Dawson's historical and educational vision, and on the other, by the institutional models of Catholic liberal arts initiatives in America. Its emergence is testimony to the enduring value of Dawson's thought and the transcendental hope of his spirit.

In the aftermath of World War II, many Western leaders and thinkers were bereft of hope as they pondered the precarious future of society in the atomic age. Dawson placed their outlook in a larger framework of understanding—a picture of truth which could only be entertained by those who believed in a God, in Chesterton's words, who knew his way out of the grave. As Dawson concluded:

> 'The irrational and amoral element in humanity has always been a factor in history, but, seen in the perspective of a few thousand years, it becomes sublimated or disinfected by time and death. But the philosopher who attempts to look directly into the mystery of iniquity, revealed in the mass movements of war and politics, can only choose between an act of despair and an act of faith.'[109]

There is no doubt as to which act governed the mind and heart of Christopher Dawson. He knew that 'civilisation is a road by which man travels, not a house for him to dwell in. His true city is elsewhere.'[110]

On the eve of his death he lapsed into a coma, but at one point he rallied and stared at a painting of the Crucifixion across from his bed. He had been unconscious for some time and could not have known what day it was. With his eyes wide open, he said simply: 'This is Trinity Sunday. I see it all and it is beautiful.'[111]

# Further reading

Any essay on Christopher Dawson is greatly indebted to the biography written by his daughter, Christina Scott, *A Historian and His World: A Life of Christopher Dawson 1889-1970* (1984). A later edition (1992) contains Dawson's autobiographical essay, *Tradition and Inheritance: Reflections on the Formative Years*, originally published in the journal, *The Wind and the Rain* (1949), and later as a booklet (1970).

John Mulloy played a vital part in fostering serious scholarship on Dawson's writings. He edited or enhanced a number of Dawson's most noteworthy books, in particular *Dynamics of World History* (1956) and *The Crisis of Western Education* (1961). From 1981 to 1995, he edited the *Dawson Newsletter*, publishing various articles by and on Dawson. A successor newsletter was published in Canada between 1997 and 2010 by Edward King on behalf of the Christopher Dawson Centre of Christian Culture. Apart from reprinting elusive Dawson articles, this newsletter provided informed commentary on the origin and context of Dawson's works.

From 2001 to 2015, the Catholic University of America Press published a series called The Works of Christopher Dawson, which comprised new editions of various Dawson books with Introductions by modern scholars such as Mary Douglas, Dermot Quinn, and George Weigel. (See: https://www.cuapress.org/author/christopher-dawson/) The General Editor of the series was Don Briel (1947-2018), who pioneered the establishment of Centers for Catholic Studies in several universities in America, beginning with the University of St Thomas in St Paul, Minnesota, where he taught for many years.

Scholarly studies of Dawson have continued to appear since his death in 1970—notably, Peter J. Cataldo (ed.), *The Dynamic Character of Christian Culture: Essays on Dawsonian Themes* (1984), Stratford Caldecott and John Morrill (eds.), *Eternity in Time: Christopher Dawson and the Catholic Idea of History* (1997), Bradley Birzer's *Sanctifying the World: The Augustinian Life and Mind of Christopher Dawson* (2007), and Joseph T. Stuart, *Christopher Dawson: A Cultural Mind in the Age of the Great War* (2022). In addition, chapters on Dawson have appeared in such books as Joseph Pearce's *Literary Converts* (1999), Adam Schwartz's *The Third Spring* (2005), and Donald J. D'Elia and Patrick Foley (eds.), *The Catholic as Historian* (2006). A major synthesis of Dawson's thought, *Christopher Dawson and the Course of Civilisations*, was produced by the American historian, James Hitchcock. While yet to be published, it contains an exhaustive bibliography of works by and on Dawson. An Australian study of Dawson has been published by the Marist theologian John Thornhill, *The Road All Peoples Travel: Christopher Dawson's Interpretation of the Cultural Developments that Ultimately Produced our Western Civilization* (2009).

The most significant Dawson archives are held by the Center for Catholic Studies at the University of St Thomas (UST) in Minnesota and the University of Notre Dame in Indiana. The UST collection comprises the bulk of Dawson's papers and manuscripts as well as his extensive personal library.

# *Endnotes*

1. "Editorial Note," *Dublin Review*, July 1940, pp.1-2.
2. Christina Scott, *A Historian and His World: A Life of Christopher Dawson 1889-1970*, 1984, p.210.
3. E.I. Watkin, "Tribute to Christopher Dawson," *Tablet* (London), 4th October 1969, p.974. Watkin was an invaluable ally to Dawson in his work as an 'interpreter.' A fellow scholar and Catholic convert—to whom Dawson ascribed, in a human sense, his own conversion—Watkin provided practical advice and intellectual encouragement as well as proof-reading and indexing of his books. In turn, Dawson deeply influenced Watkin's thought and writings.
4. Bernard Wall, *Headlong into Change: an Autobiography and a Memoir of Ideas since the Thirties*, 1969, p.89.
5. E.I. Watkin, "Christopher Dawson," *Commonweal*, 27th October 1933, p.607. A large part of this article was republished in a memoir of Dawson edited by M.D. Knowles and drawn from the *Proceedings of the British Academy*, Vol.LVII, 1973.
6. This essay was later reprinted as a chapter in John J. Mulloy (ed.), *Dynamics of World History*, 1956.
7. This two-part autobiographical essay first appeared in two issues of the English journal, *The Wind and the Rain* (Spring & Summer 1949) and was later reprinted as a booklet - in America in 1970, and in England in 1989 under the title, *Memories of a Victorian Childhood*. It has most recently been

republished as part of the new edition of Christina Scott's biography (1992).

8. Watkin, 1933, p.607.

9. "Tradition and Inheritance," p.19.

10. *Ibid.,* p.20.

11. Goffin, *op.cit.,* p.129.

12. "Frank Sheed Talks with Christopher Dawson," *Sign* (USA), December 1958, p.34.

13. Frank Sheed, *The Church and I*, 1974, p.124.

14. *Understanding Europe*, 1952, p.245.

15. *Movement of World Revolution*, 1959, pp.62, 66.

16. Goffin, *op.cit.*, p.41.

17. Scott, *op.cit.*, p.40. Dawson's appreciation of German culture is evident in *Progress and Religion* (1929), pp.25-27, where he describes the intellectual awakening of the late 18th and early 19th centuries, as expressed in the literature of Goethe, the music of Mozart and Beethoven, and the philosophy of Kant, and sees the German view of life as 'musical rather than mathematical.' See also his *Understanding Europe* (1952; new ed.2009) for two illuminating sections on German history (chapter IV, "Germany and Central Europe," and chapter X, "Intellectual Antecedents: Hegel and the German Ideology.")

18. *Enquiries into Religion and Culture*, 1933, p.v.

19. "Catholic Sociology," *Spectator* (London), 12th February 1943, p.152.

20. M.D. Knowles (ed.), "Christopher Dawson 1889-1970," *Proceedings of the British Academy*, 1973, p.442.

21. "Why I am a Catholic," *Catholic Times* (London), 21st May 1926, p.11.

22. *The Making of Europe: An Introduction to the History of European Unity,* 1932, pp.49-50.

23. The essays that Dawson contributed to *A Monument to St Augustine* (1930) were republished under the title, "St

Augustine and his Age," in the book of essays, *Enquiries into Religion and Culture*, 1933.

24. Aidan Nichols OP, "Christopher Dawson's Catholic Setting," in Stratford Caldecott and John Morrill (eds.), *Eternity in Time: Christopher Dawson and the Catholic Idea of History*, 1997, p.34.

25. "Why I am a Catholic," p.11.

26. Scott, *op.cit.*, pp.66-7.

27. "The Nature and Destiny of Man" first appeared in a symposium edited by Fr. Cuthbert, *God and the Supernatural: a Catholic Statement of the Christian Faith*, 1920, and was republished as a chapter of *Enquiries into Religion and Culture*, 1933.

28. Russell Hittinger, "Christopher Dawson: A View from the Social Sciences," in *The Catholic Writer: Proceedings of the Wethersfield Institute 1989*, 1991, p.33.

29. "Tradition and Inheritance," p.31.

30. "The Problem of Metahistory," in *Dynamics of World History*, 1956, p.287.

31. *The Dividing of Christendom*, 1965, p.15.

32. Scott, *op.cit.*, p.49.

33. Martin Haley, "Christopher Dawson: a great scholar, writer, historian," *Advocate* (Melbourne), 2nd July 1970, p.17.

34. *The Age of the Gods: A Study in the origins of Culture in Prehistoric Europe and the Ancient East*, 1928, p.22.

35. *Antiquity*, December 1928, p.485.

36. *Progress and Religion: An Historical Enquiry*, 1929, pp.viii, 228.

37. For example, Dawson later interpreted Communism as a substitute religious faith. In *Religion and the Modern State*, 1936, p.58: '... Russian Communism does resemble a religion in many respects. Its attitude ... [is that] of a believer to the gospel of salvation; Lenin is more than a political hero, he is

the canonized saint of Communism ...; and the Communist ethic is religious in its absoluteness and its unlimited claims to the spiritual allegiance of its followers.'

38. *Religion and the Rise of Western Culture*, 1950, p.7.

39. *Religion and Culture*, 1948, p.83.

40. *Progress and Religion*, 1929, pp.117-121. See also Clement Anthony, "The Unpublished Second Volume," *Dawson Newsletter*, Spring 1990, pp.14-16.

41. Scott, *op.cit.*, pp.109-11.

42. Christopher Dawson, General Introduction to Essays in Order, in Jacques Maritain, *Religion and Culture*, 1931, p.x.

43. The authors from various European countries included Jacques Maritain (France), Peter Wust and Carl Schmitt (Germany), Nicholas Berdyaev (Russia), and E.I. Watkin and Herbert Read (England).

44. "Catholicism and the Bourgeois Mind," in *Dynamics of World History*, 1956, p.206.

45. *The Modern Dilemma: the Problem of European Unity*, 1932, pp.112-13.

46. A present-day historian, Fernando Cervantes of Bristol University, has noted Dawson's pioneering awareness of the importance of the Northern barbarians to the formation of European civilisation. See Fernando Cervantes, "Christopher Dawson and Europe," in *Eternity in Time, op.cit.*, p.58.

47. Aldous Huxley, "Historical Generalizations," in *The Olive Tree and Other Essays*, 1936, pp.130.

48. *The Making of Europe*, 1932, p.17.

49. C.J. McNaspy SJ, private letter to author, 7th June 1972.

50. Major excerpts from *The Making of Europe* were included in the Random House booklet, "Christianity in the Roman Empire: Why Did It Succeed?," 1967, and in the D.C. Heath publication, Thomas W. Africa et al. (eds.), *Critical Issues in History* , 1967, under the title, "The Carolingian Empire as an

Embodiment of Christian Idealism."

51. "The Interracial Cooperation as a Factor in European Culture," 1933, p. 9. This was an address to a conference in Rome in 1932 on the theme of "Europe", organised by the Royal Academy of Italy. It is fully discussed in Scott, *op.cit.*, pp.104-7.

52. Dawson revealed an early fascination with the history of China, as documented by Edward King, "China in the Thought of Christopher Dawson," *Dawson Newsletter*, Spring 1989, pp.5-10.

53. "Christianity and Sex," in *Enquiries*, 1933, pp.259-291. See also James Hitchcock, "To Tear Down and To Build Up: Christianity and the Subversive Forces in Western Civilization," in *Christianity and Western Civilization: papers presented at a conference sponsored by the Wethersfield Institute*, New York City, 15th October 1995, pp.57-71.

54. *Historic Reality of Christian Culture: a Way to the Renewal of Human Life*, 1960, pp.71-2; *Enquiries*, 1933, pp.168-9. See also John J. Mulloy, "Islam's Relationship to Judaism and Christianity," *Dawson Newsletter*, Fall 1985, pp.14-15.

55. *The Spirit of the Oxford Movement*, 1933, pp.63-4, 132.

56. *The Formation of Christendom*, 1967, pp.7-8.

57. The Spirit of the Oxford Movement, 1933, pp.ix, 3.

58. "Newman and the Sword of the Spirit," *Sword of the Spirit*, August 1945. Reprinted in *Dawson Newsletter*, Spring-Summer 1991, pp.12-13.

59. *Religion and the Modern State*, 1936, p.140.

60. *The Formation of Christendom*, 1967, p.15.

61. *The Modern Dilemma*, 1932, p.109.

62. *Medieval Essays*, 1953, pp.73-4. See also John J. Mulloy, "Medieval Studies and the Challenge of Christian Culture," *Dawson Newsletter*, Summer 1983, pp. 4-5.

63. Controversy has surrounded the attitudes of Catho-

lic writers in the 1930s, especially in relation to Fascism and Communism, and Dawson was embroiled to some extent in these debates. See Scott, *op.cit.*, pp.122-27, for a useful analysis, and her letter in the *Chesterton Review,* August 1999, pp.405-7, in response to a symposium on this topic, "Fascism and British Catholic Writers," *Chesterton Review*, February/May 1999, pp.21-79.

    64. *Religion and the Modern State*, 1936, p.106.

    65. *Ibid.*, p.105.

    66. *Ibid.*, viii.

    67. Bernard Wall, "Christopher Dawson—A Lion in Fight against Half-truth," *Catholic Herald* (London), 29th May 1970.

    68. *Beyond Politics*, 1939, pp. 130-31.

    69. *Ibid.*

    70. Scott, *op.cit.*, p.137.

    71. *The Judgement of the Nations*, 1943, p.vi.

    72. *Ibid.*, pp.102-03.

    73. Religion and Culture, 1948, p.50. Gerald Russello has noted that anthropological scholars such as Rebecca French and David Hollinger have made clear that religious interpretations of the world remain the dominant way in which people understand reality. See Gerald Russello, "The Relevance of Christopher Dawson: a review of *Progress and Religion*," *First Things*, April 2002, p.48.

    74. *Ibid.*, pp.49-50.

    75. *Ibid.*, p.49.

    76. "Christopher Dawson," *Tablet* (London), 6th June 1970, p.558.

    77. "Ploughing a Lone Furrow," in J. Stanley Murphy (ed.), *Christianity and Culture*, 1960, p.17.

    78. Christopher Dawson, Introduction to M. O'Leary, *The Catholic Church and Education*, 1943, p.vii.

    79. *Ibid.*, p.ix.

80. The two articles were: "Education and the Crisis of Christian Culture," *Lumen Vitae: International Review of Religious Education,* April 1946, pp.204-215, and "The Study of Christian Culture as a Means of Education," *Lumen Vitae,* Jan-March 1950, pp.171-186.

81. *Progress and Religion,* 1929, p.167.

82. Joseph Cardinal Ratzinger, *Europe Today and Tomorrow: Addressing the Fundamental Issues,* 2007, p.23. Bradley Birzer has remarked on the similarity of the arguments and the language between Dawson and Pope Benedict XVI, especially in the Pope's *Christianity and the Crisis of Cultures* (2006). See "Rediscovering Christopher Dawson: An Interview with Dr Bradley J. Birzer," www.ignatiusinsight.com/features 2008/bbirzer_interview_feb08.asp. Other writers on contemporary Europe who have recognised the value of Dawson's writings are David Gress, in *From Plato to Nato: The Idea of the West and Its Opponents* (1998), and George Weigel, in his Introduction to a new edition of *Understanding Europe* (2009).

83. Dermot Quinn, Introduction, *Dynamics of World History,* 2002, ISI Books edition, p.xii.

84. *Dawson Newsletter,* Fall 1981, p.2.

85. *The Crisis of Western Education,* 1961, p.188.

86. *The Movement of World Revolution,* 1959, p.79.

87. "Tradition and Inheritance," pp.31-2.

88. Chauncey Stillman, "Christopher Dawson: Recollections from America," in Peter J. Cataldo (ed.), *The Dynamic Character of Christian Culture,* 1984, pp.217-22.

89. "Transfusion at Harvard," *Newsweek,* 25th April 1955, p.56.

90. "Christianity at Harvard," *Time,* 23rd June 1958, p.36.

91. *The Formation of Christendom,* 1967, p.16.

92. *The Judgement of the Nations,* 1943, p.123.

93. "Catholic Culture in America," *Critic* (USA), June-Ju-

ly 1959, pp.7, 59. Dawson first spelt out his insights into the uniqueness of American history and culture in *Understanding Europe* (1952; new ed. 2009), chapter IX: "Europe Overseas: The New World of America."

94. "Professor Dawson Speaks Out on Church, State and Religious Education in America: an interview with Michael Novak," *Jubilee* (USA), April 1961, p.27.

95. *The Historic Reality of Christian Culture*, 1960, p.77.

96. *Ibid.*, pp.29-30.

97. *Religion and the Modern State*, 1936, pp.146-7.

98. *America and the Secularization of Modern Culture*. The Smith History Lecture, 1960, University of St Thomas, Houston, Texas, pp.30-1. Dawson's conclusion in 1960 echoed his observation in 1925 in a journal article, "Religion and the Life of Civilizations," republished as a chapter in *Dynamics*, 1956: "A society which has lost its religion becomes sooner or later a society which has lost its culture." (p.132)

99. *The Spirit of the Oxford Movement*, 1933, p.135.

100. *The Formation of Christendom*, 1967, p.18.

101. E.I. Watkin, "Reflections on the Work of Christopher Dawson," *Downside Review*, January 1971, p.10.

102. Fernando Cervantes, "A Vision to Regain? Reconsidering Christopher Dawson," *New Blackfriars*, October 1989, p.142.

103. Dermot Quinn, "Christopher Dawson and the Catholic Idea of History," in *Eternity in Time, op.cit.*, p.76.

104. Bernard Wall, *op.cit.*, 1970.

105. John J. Mulloy, *The Wanderer* (USA), 4th December 1975, p.5.

106. *The Gods of Revolution*, 1972, pp.132-3, 147.

107. *The Movement of World Revolution*, 1959, p.179.

108. Daniel Callahan, "Christopher Dawson at Harvard," *Commonweal*, 15th June 1962, p.294.

109. "The Pessimism of Dr Toynbee," *Tablet* (London), 18th December 1948, p.404.
110. *Religion and the Modern State*, 1936, p.xv.
111. Scott, *op.cit.*, p.207.

www.ingramcontent.com/pod-product-compliance
Lightning Source LLC
Chambersburg PA
CBHW030303010526
44107CB00053B/1800